POPULAR PIANO SOLOS

Pop Hits, Broadway, Movies and More!

ISBN 978-1-4234-0908-3

EXCLUSIVELY DISTRIBUTED BY

7777 W. BLUEMOUND RD. P.O. BOX 13819 MILWAUKEE, WI 53213

Visit Hal Leonard Online at
www.halleonard.com

Contents

Cabaret
from the Musical CABARET

Words by Fred Ebb
Music by John Kander
Arranged by Eric Baumgartner

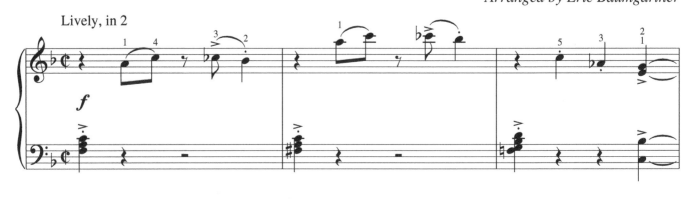

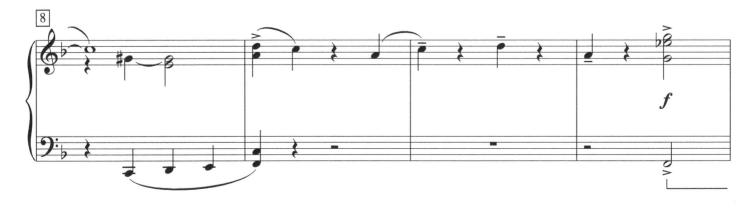

Under the Sea
from Walt Disney's THE LITTLE MERMAID

Lyrics by Howard Ashman
Music by Alan Menken
Arranged by Eric Baumgartner

What a Wonderful World

Words and Music by George David Weiss
and Bob Thiele
Arranged by Eric Baumgartner

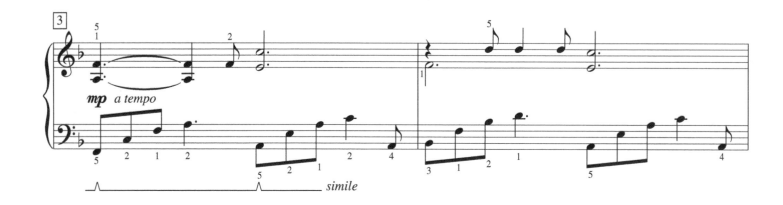

Let It Be

Words and Music by John Lennon
and Paul McCartney
Arranged by Eric Baumgartner

Gently, with a Gospel feel

p sempre legato

With sparse pedal throughout

Puttin' On the Ritz
from the Motion Picture PUTTIN' ON THE RITZ

Words and Music by
Irving Berlin
Arranged by Eric Baumgartner

Très sophistiqué

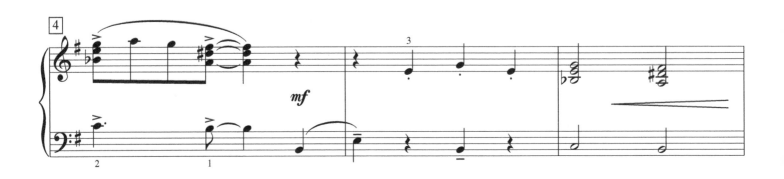

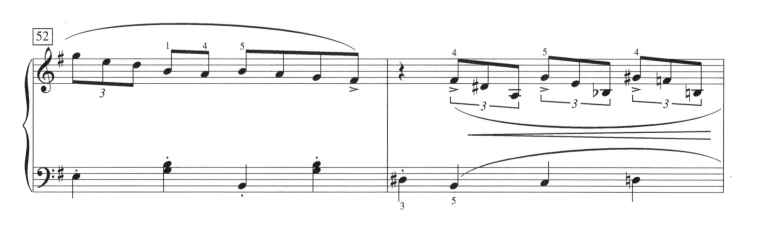

D.S. al Coda

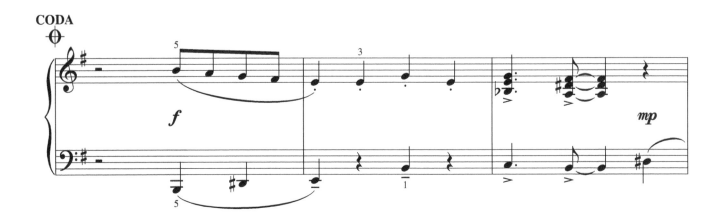

In the Mood

By Joe Garland
Arranged by Eric Baumgartner

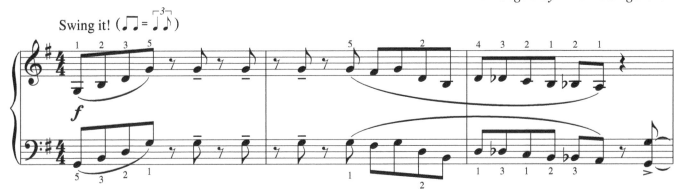

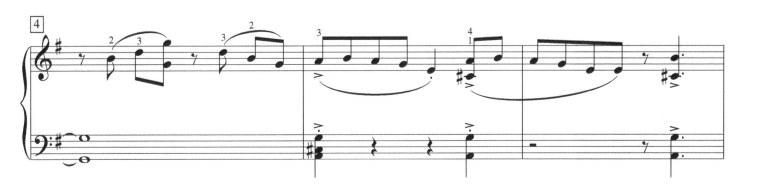

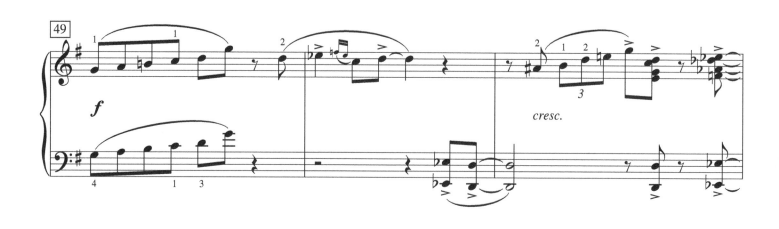

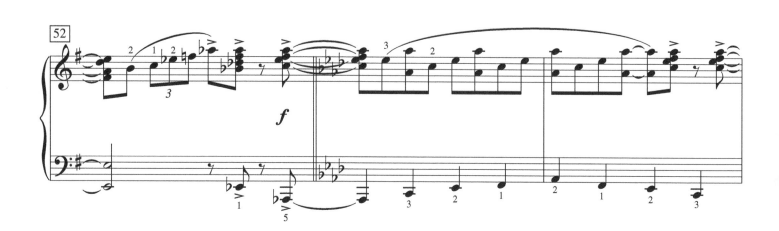

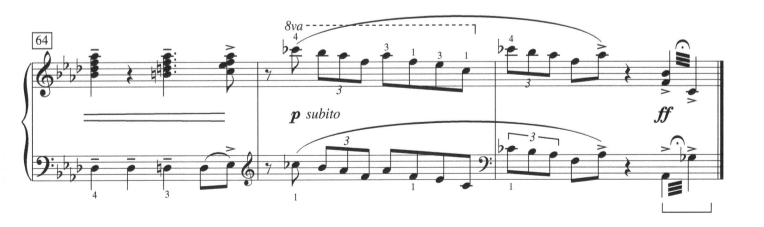

Be Our Guest
from Walt Disney's BEAUTY AND THE BEAST

Lyrics by Howard Ashman
Music by Alan Menken
Arranged by Eric Baumgartner

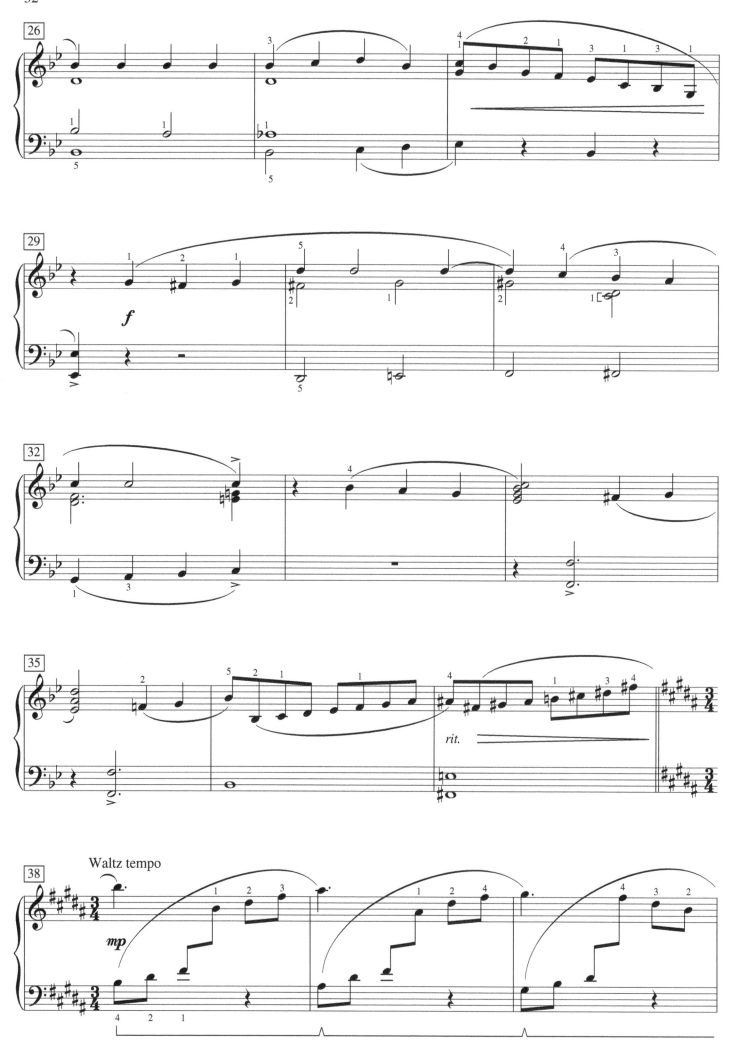

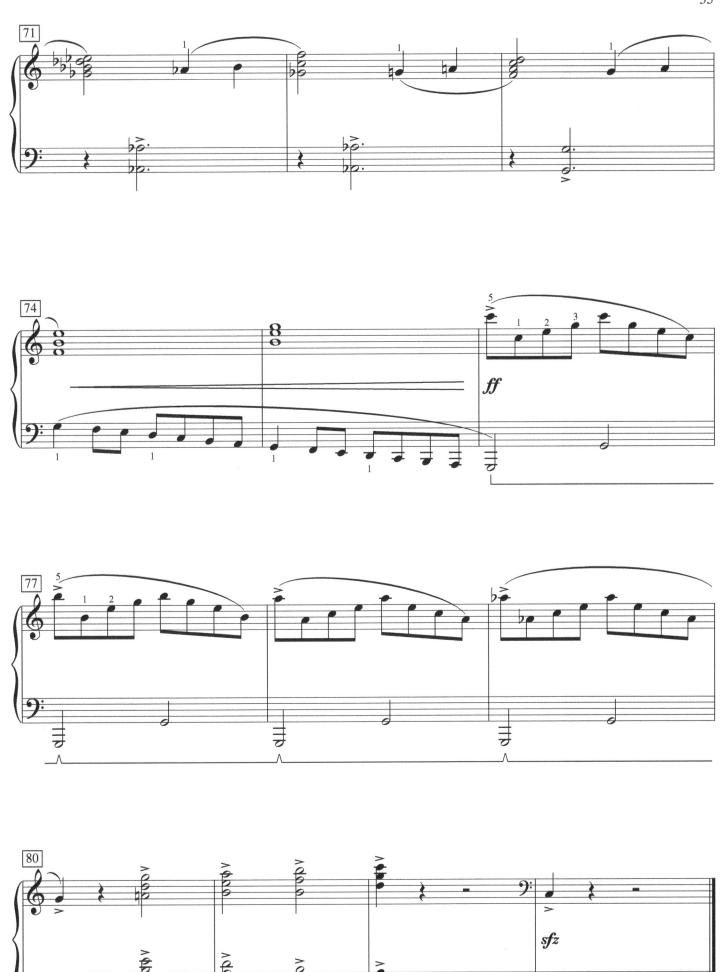

Georgia on My Mind

Words by Stuart Gorrell
Music by Hoagy Carmichael
Arranged by Eric Baumgartner

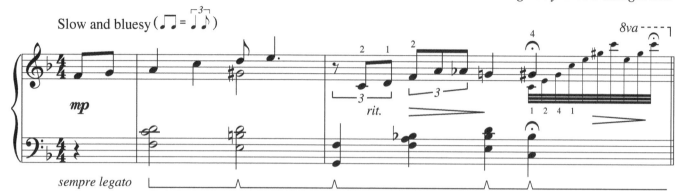

(continue pedal judiciously!)

Playfully *(slightly faster)*

detached (no pedal)

Linus and Lucy

By Vince Guaraldi
Arranged by Eric Baumgartner

The Way You Look Tonight
from SWING TIME

Words by Dorothy Fields
Music by Jerome Kern
Arranged by Eric Baumgartner

Freely, with great warmth

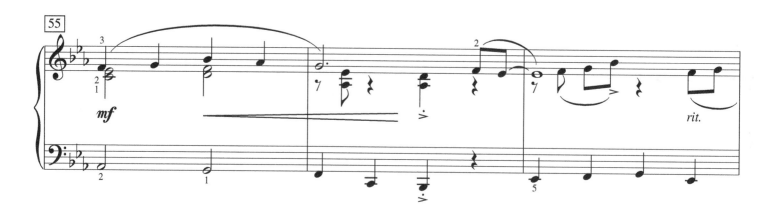